A Note to Parents and Teachers

DK Readers is a compelling program for beginning readers, designed in conjunction with leading literacy experts, including Dr. Linda Gambrell, director of the Eugene T. Moore School of Education, Clemson University, and past president of the National Reading Conference.

Beautiful illustrations and superb full-color photographs combine with engaging, easy-to-read stories to offer a fresh approach to each subject in the series. Each DK READER is guaranteed to capture a child's interest while developing his or her reading skills, general knowledge, and love of reading.

The five levels of DK READERS are aimed at different reading abilities, enabling you to choose the books that are exactly right for your children:

Pre-Level 1 – Learning to read
Level 1 – Beginning to read
Level 2 – Beginning to read alone
Level 3 – Reading alone
Level 4 – Proficient readers

The "normal" age at which a child begins to read can be anywhere from three to eight years old, so these levels are only a general guideline.

No matter which level you select, you can be sure that you are helping your child learn to read, then read to learn!

LONDON, NEW YORK, MUNICH,
MELBOURNE, AND DELHI

Editor Elizabeth Hester
Senior Designer Tai Blanche
Assistant Managing Art Editor Michelle B
Publishing Director Beth Sutinis
Creative Director Tina Vaughan
DTP Designer Milos Orlovic
Production Ivor Parker

Reading Consultant
Linda Gambrell, Ph.D.

Produced by
Shoreline Publishing Group LLC
President James Buckley, Jr.
Art Director Tom Carling
Carling Design, Inc.

Produced in partnership and licensed by I
League Baseball Properties, Inc.
**Vice President of Publishing
and MLB Photos:** Don Hintze

First American Edition, 2005
05 06 07 08 09 10 9 8 7 6 5 4 3 2 1
Published in the United States by DK Publishing, Inc.
375 Hudson St., New York, NY 10014

A catalog record is available from the Library of Congress.
ISBN 0-7566-1207-1 (Paperback) 0-7566-1206-3 (Hardcover)

Color reproduction by Colourscan, Singapore
Printed and bound in China by L. Rex Printing Co., Ltd.

Photography credits:
All photographs by Mike Eliason.
Baseball shoe photo on page 13 courtesy of Reebok.

*Thanks to the Michael Martinez, Eric Kay,
and the Anaheim Angels for their gracious cooperation
in the making of this book.*

Discover more at
www.dk.com

BEGINNING
TO READ ALONE
2

A Batboy's Day

Written by James Buckley, Jr.

DK

My name is Michael Martinez.
I have one of the coolest jobs
in the world.
I am a batboy for the Anaheim
Angels baseball team!
A batboy makes sure baseball
players have all the gear they need.

I do a lot of important
jobs to help the
Angels play their best

About six hours
before the game,
I arrive at the team's
home at Angel Stadium.

4

The Angels cannot do their jobs without their bats.

I help carry the bats from a storage room to the dugout.

I carry bats in this sunflower-seed bucket.

The bats are stored in racks during games. Each player has his own bats.

Labeling bats

Players put their uniform number on the knob of the bat. These bats belong to catcher Josh Paul.

Next I fill up the helmet racks.
Then I lay out the batting gloves
that some players use when hitting.

The catcher's gear goes into the
dugout racks, too.

Being a bat boy is certainly fun.
But it's hard work, too.
I even have to do laundry!
I help clean the players' warm-up
jerseys, game uniforms, and towels.

Huge washing machines help me
get this job done quickly.

I lay out a row of towels in the dugout before the game. Players use them to wipe sweat from their faces or pine tar from their hands. Then I put out pine-tar rags for the batters to use.

Pine tar

Players use a special rag to wipe this super sticky stuff onto their bat handles. It gives their hands a better grip on the bats.

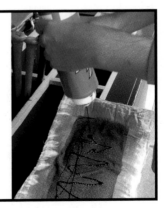

I finish up my
work in the
dugout.

Now it is time
to get the bull pens ready.
The bull pens are located behind
the outfield fence.
Bull pens are where the
pitchers warm up before
they play.
I put out towels, water,
and snacks for our pitchers.

There sure is a lot to do!
I get to drive a cart to help me

get it all done quickly.

Now I go to the batting cages.
These are areas beneath the fans'
seats where players warm up before
and during the game.
I put out baseballs and batting tees
for the players to use.

Baseball players don't dress in a locker room.
They dress in the "clubhouse."

One of my jobs is to take care of the clubhouse.

I make sure each player has all their Angels clothing in their dressing area. That means a jersey, pants, socks, T-shirts, and caps.

Baseball players like to wear clean and shiny shoes called "spikes." The other batboys and I shine a lot of those spikes!

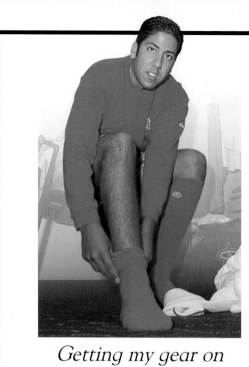
Getting my gear on

Game time is now less than an hour away! It's time for me to get dressed.

Angels batboys wear uniforms like the players. We have our own dressing area. I even have my own glove!

I put on my socks, pants, and white uniform jersey.

My own personal glove!

t is important for us
o look neat and
clean when we
are on the field.

We all want fans
o watch us do
a good job, and
we try to look
ike pros.

Here I am on the
Angel Stadium field,
ready and waiting for
the game to begin.
How do I look?

Before the game starts, I make
one last check of the dugout.
Are all the bats ready?
Are the helmets in place?
Do the players have all the water
and snacks they'll need?

OK, it looks good.
Now it's time to play
the game!

This is my view from
where I sit.
I'm closer to home
plate than the pitcher!

This is a great way
o watch a ball game!

have to remind myself that I'm
here to work, not to look around.
must pay close attention to the
jame at all times.

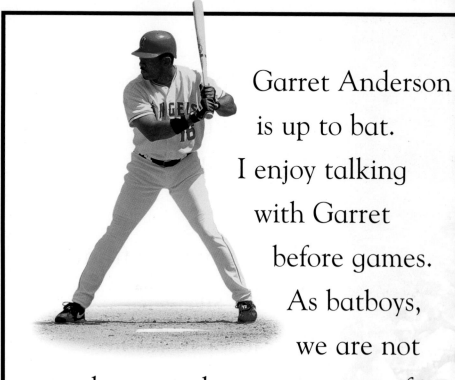

Garret Anderson is up to bat. I enjoy talking with Garret before games. As batboys, we are not on the team, but we are part of it.

The players are so nice, it's like working with 25 good friends.

I root for Garret to get a hit. After he finishes his at-bat, it is my job to run out to home plate and pick up his bat.

know that people are watching
me, so I try to do my job quickly
and without tripping!

I put Garrett's bat back in the rack
and get ready for the next hitter.

Angels players are not the only people on the field that we help. As the home team, we take care of the umpires, too. On hot days, we bring them water if they need it.

It's hot today!

We also make sure they have enough baseballs. When the home-plate umpire needs more, we run out and deliver the special game balls.

This is one of my favorite moments
as a batboy.

One of our players has just hit
a home run!

As he circles the bases and the
crowd cheers, I pick up his bat.

Then I run back to the dugout.

I give the hitter a high-five.

Way to go, Angels!

Then he heads to the dugout to
slap hands with his teammates.

One of the best things about being a batboy with the Angels is that I get to work with my brother!

Raymond is also a batboy.
He started before me and helped me meet the people who gave me my job.
I love having him around.
He helps me do the job right, and makes work even more fun!

My brother and me at the ballpark

Together, Raymond and I have
seen a lot of exciting baseball
moments, such as David Eckstein
making this great play as shortstop.
David is one of my best friends
on the Angels.
I love to see him in action!

As soon as the game ends, my work begins again!
Remember all that gear I put out before the game?

Now it is time to put it away.

I start by cleaning the dugout.

I love working with the Angels, but these guys can be kind of messy.

There are sunflower seeds and water cups everywhere!

I drink some water and then I grab the broom. I load the towels into the laundry basket and take the gear back to the storage room.

I also drive to the bull pen to clean up out there.

I pack up all the bats and take them back inside.
I follow the long tunnel that goes under the stands to the clubhouse.

Next we batboys work on the clubhouse. It gets pretty messy here, too!

Packing dinner for the food bank

We get to eat dinner with the players after games. A different kind of meal is served each night.
After we eat, I clean up the dishes and the leftovers.
The extra food is donated to local food banks.

Now all the gear is put away,
the clubhouse is tidied up, and
the dugout is clean.
My work is finished for the day.

I've been at the
ballpark for
almost 12
hours, and
I've loved
every minute!

Before I leave,
I enter a code
in a clock that
counts my
work hours.

Now it's time to go home.
My truck is parked in the Angel
Stadium parking lot, near the
big red "A" for "Angels."

I leave the stadium behind for now.
I can't wait to do it all over
again next game!

How to Become a Batboy (or Batgirl!)

Major League batboys must be 16 years old, but those are not the only teams that need batboys. First, of course, you don't have to be a boy. Many minor-league or college teams choose girls to help with their equipment on the field. Different teams have different rules about age. The best way to find out what a team's rules are is just to ask!

Here are some types of baseball teams you can try to work for: minor-league teams, semipro or summer-league teams, college teams, high-school teams, American Legion teams, or "club" teams. Don't forget other youth-league teams, too.

Find the mailing address of a team near you. Ask your parents to help you write a letter like the example shown below. (Remember, many kids like you want these jobs, so you have a lot of competition!)

Dear [name of team's general manager],

I'm a big fan of [team name here] and of baseball. I would like to find out how I can become a batboy/batgirl for your club. Can you let me know? I'm a hard worker. I'm very dependable. I hope you will give me a chance.

Thank you!

Then sign your name and make sure to include your return address.

Good luck!

LEARNING
DISABILITIES
AND ADHD